About the Book

This book is about the rock cycle (the unending breaking down and building up of rock). Would you believe that the slate walk around your house was once mud, that a marble statue was once crushed shell under the ocean, that deserts and sandbanks were scoured from rock?

Slowly but surely rock breaks down and rebuilds — from the drift of eroded sand to violent volcanoes and rocking earthquakes to the rebuilding of rock mountains and reshaping of earth crust.

We can find many places where the forces of the weather cycle and rock cycle work together to make an environment suitable for living things or destructive to them. The more we understand these forces, the better able we are to protect our environment and ourselves.

ROCK
ALL
AROUND

by Margaret Farrington Bartlett

Illustrated by John Kaufmann

Coward-McCann, Inc.   New York

General Editor: Margaret Farrington Bartlett
Consultant: Theodore D. Johnson
Montclair Public Schools

1578560

ROCK ALL AROUND

When you walk along a brook,
you find rock in many places —
a high cliff,
boulders in a brook,
or pebbles on a sandy shore.
The cliff, boulders, pebbles and sand
are all made from rock.

A crust of rock covers the whole earth.
You have seen a flat crust on a pie.
The crust of the earth is not flat.
It goes around the earth like the strong cover
you see around your baseball.

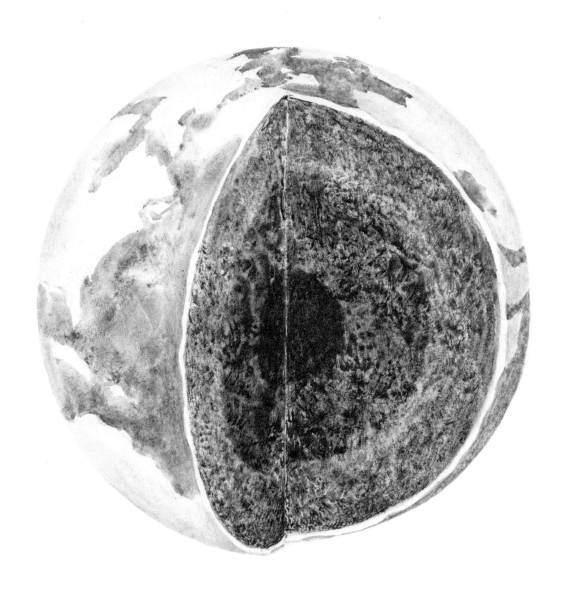

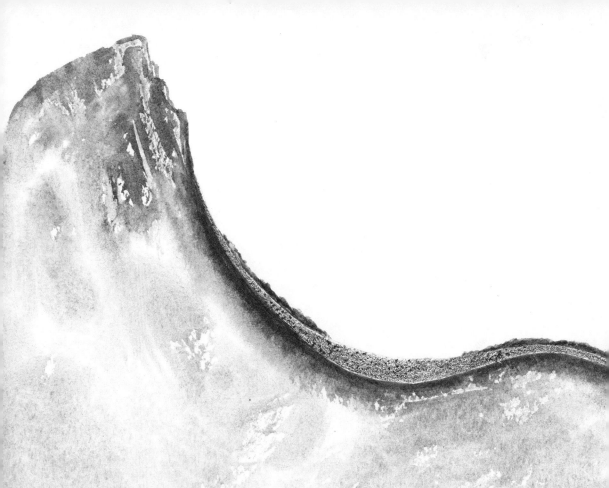

You can see the crust on the tops of many mountains.
There it is not covered by soil.
A little way down the mountainside
a thin carpet of soil may hide the crust.
In the valley, it may take a bulldozer
to push away the thick carpet of soil
that has collected over the crust.

Even under the ocean
there is rock crust under layers
that make up the ocean floor —
sand and silt made of mud and clay,
mixed with ooze filled with skeletons
of tiny animals and plants.

The story of rock goes back
to the beginning of the earth.
Many scientists believe
there was a time when all rock
was like a thick hot melted rock soup.
Some of the rock soup cooled
and made a crust around the earth.

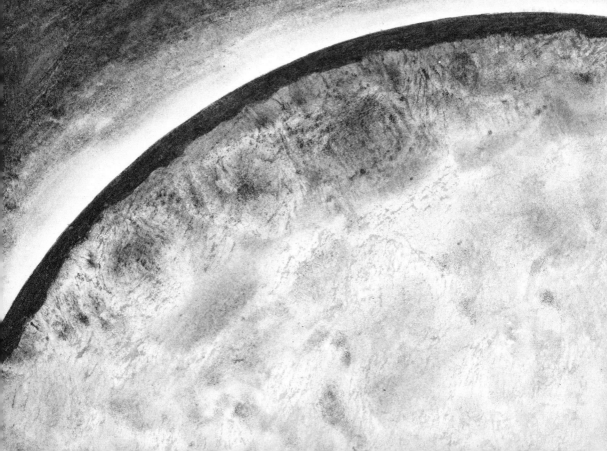

Have you ever watched a pot of vegetable soup
boil and bubble?
Vegetable bits move around and around.
Some float at the top.
Heavier bits go to the bottom
and boil over and over.
When the soup cools,
you may see bits of vegetables
trapped through the skin or crust that forms.

The rock soup of the earth
was not made of vegetables.
It was made of minerals.
As the crust formed,
it trapped many minerals
that are useful, such as
iron, talc, tin, salt, copper, silver and gold.

iron

talc

tin

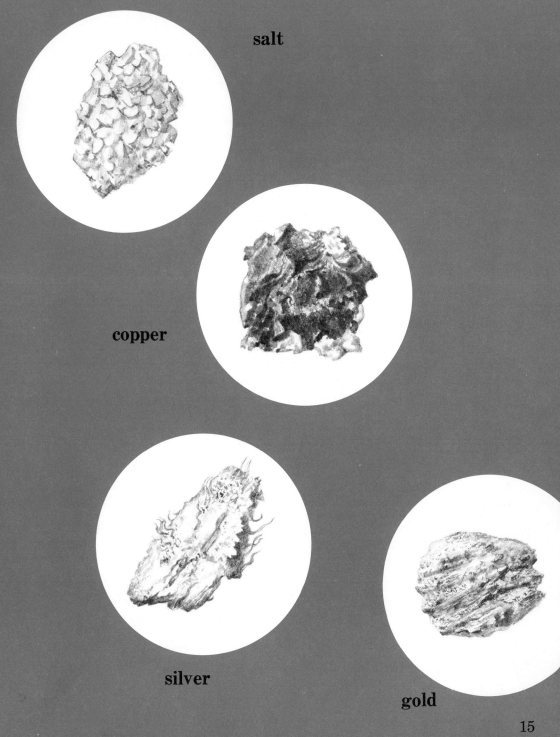

salt

copper

silver

gold

Some minerals in rock are hard, as iron or copper.
Some break easily, as chalk or talc.
Some of the minerals are washed and scrubbed
from rock by rain and rivers.

When so much water mixes with a mineral
that it seems to disappear,
we say that the mineral is *dissolved*.

Salt is one mineral that is dissolved
and carried to the ocean by rivers.
You cannot see the dissolved salt in the ocean,
but you can taste it.

When minerals are dissolved from rock,
it crumbles.
Slowly the rock changes.
Along a brook you can find many places
where rock is being crumbled and changed
by plants and weather.

When rain, snow, wind and sun beat against a cliff, they soften minerals, and loose pieces of rock crumble.

Water settles in cracks, and when it freezes,
the ice spreads and takes up more room.
Cracks grow bigger and pieces fall from the cliff.

You can find pieces broken
from the weathered cliff.

Have you ever felt heat
from rock or sand on your bare feet?
The sun's heat makes rock stretch a little
and cold winds make rock shrink a little.
This makes flakes of rock chip off.
You cannot see the rock stretch and shrink,
but often you can find loosened flakes on the rock.

Small plants grow from cracks in the weathered cliff.
Plant roots eat into the rock,
feeding on minerals.
As roots spread and grow bigger,
the cracks grow bigger.
Chips and flakes fall to the ground.

In the brook you can see
where rock is changed by other rock.
Brook water washes over pebbles.
The water's force pushes some pebbles along.

Pebbles rub against pebbles.
They grind over sand and bang against boulders.
Big and small pebbles chip, wear and grow smaller.
Sift tiny pebbles and sand through your fingers.
Feel the hard grains
and see the colored bits of minerals.

Broken rock, sand and pebbles,
together with mud and clay from weathered minerals,
make a kind of rock rubbish.
It is called *sediment*.
Sediment does not stay in one place.
It shifts and wears away or *erodes*.
It slides down the slopes of hills to brooks and rivers.
Plants, leaves and dust of old bones
wash from banks and add to the sediment.
Every day huge loads are carried down
into the ocean by brooks and rivers.
One layer is covered by another and another
until many layers press together under the ocean.

While old rock is breaking down,
new rock is being made.
While high places erode,
other places build up.

Many scientists believe that erosion
helps make the beginnings of new mountains.
As the old mountain erodes,
more loads of sediment collect under the ocean.
As the huge load presses down,
it makes other material push up.

When you step in soft mud,
the force of your foot presses down into a footprint.
This makes other mud push up around it.
The down-and-up motions make new high places.

Motion inside the earth
changes the crust too.
This motion may be the beginning
of an earthquake or a volcano.

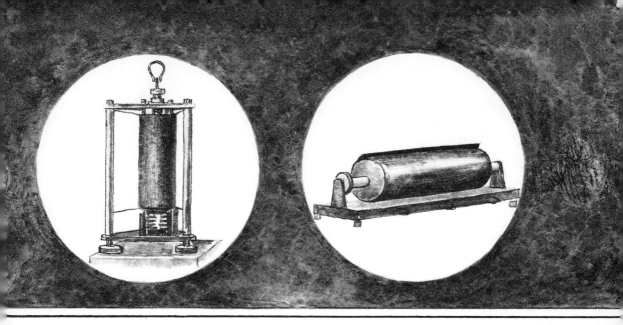

earthquake motion

Scientists have not been able to explore
far inside the earth.
But they do have special tools
that signal warnings of motion
from under the crust.
The motion may be very slight
or it may warn of an earthquake so violent
that the crust cracks, heaves and twists.

It is as if waves like ocean waves
were traveling through the earth.
Some waves travel back and forth like ripples
when you drop a pebble in a pool.

Some waves travel up and down from the crust
toward the center of the earth and back again.

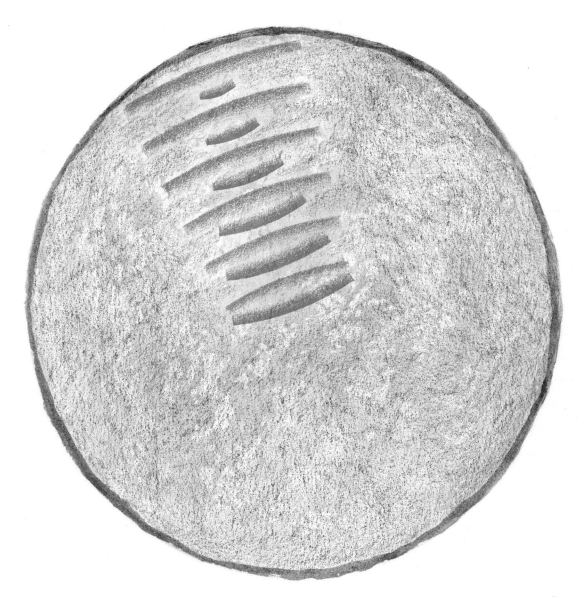

Waves of rock push with tremendous force.
The crust wrinkles and buckles.
It cracks and one side may tilt up or sink lower.

More jolts may move broken blocks of crust higher
and slowly shape new mountains and mountain chains.

As the crust jolts and wrinkles,
layers of sediment squeeze together tighter.
Sediment slides into hollows, pushes into cracks
or may be crushed and buried under other sediment.

Slowly year after year
water seeps through the sediment
and dissolved minerals cement it together.
This makes new rock from old eroded rock.
It is called *sedimentary* rock.

Signals from inside the earth may warn of a volcano
that can change the crust and make new rock.
Under the earth's crust
is a very thick layer of rock material.
It may hold pockets of more thick hot melted
rock soup called *magma*.

Or a violent explosion may force
hot rock, steam and ashes
through the crust and high into the air.
This exploded magma is called *lava*.
It may fall onto the earth and harden
as it makes new rock and slowly builds
new high places.
Rock made of hot magma from inside the earth
is called *igneous* rock.

Rock that is under great heat
or squeezed under tremendous pressure
can change into a different kind of rock.
Then it is called *metamorphic* rock.

Rock exploded into the air from a volcano
may fall back into hot magma
and be melted again
or move deep into the earth
and mix with other minerals.

Rock may be changed so many times
that it is impossible to tell
what kind of rock it was first.

sand

sandstone

As you learn more about rock,
you can easily imagine
that sandstone was once sand.
But you may find it hard to believe
that the slate walk around your house
was once mud or clay
or that the marble counter in the drugstore
was once a mass of shell under the ocean.
Slate and marble are both metamorphic rock
and have changed more than once.

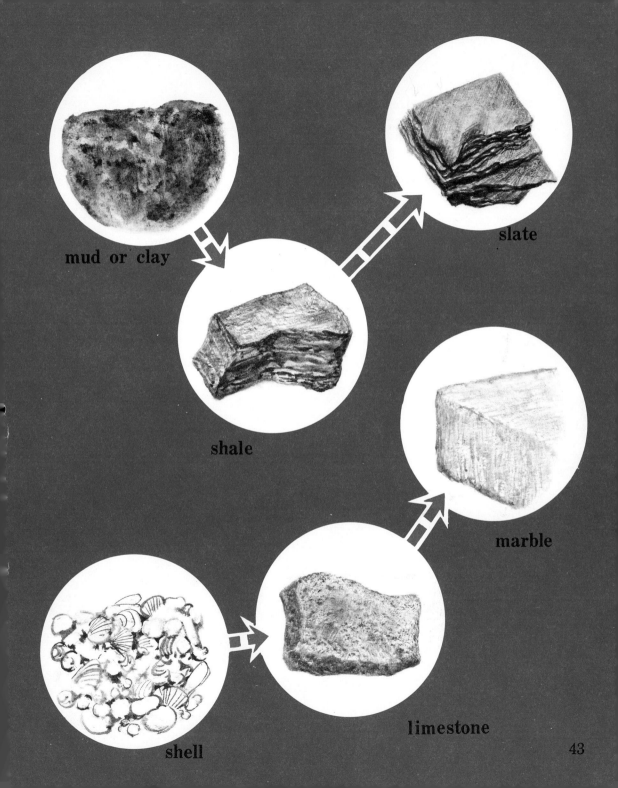

mud or clay

shale

slate

shell

limestone

marble

From the time that it was formed,
the earth's crust has been changing.
Rock rubbish becomes sedimentary rock.

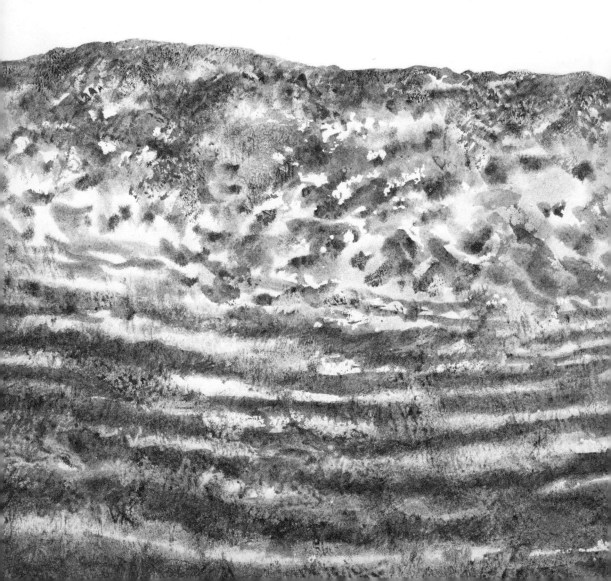

Hot magma from under the crust
builds new igneous rock.
Old rock can change and make metamorphic rock.

45

Mountain, cliff, boulder,
and pebble weather and erode,
but the strong crust keeps on building.
This is happening wherever you find rock.